# Westward to Oregon

Patricia Pfitsch

Illustrated by John English

Rigby

Lizzie sat beside Papa on the seat of their wagon. The mountains made a purple smudge on the horizon. The wagon train had been traveling all summer, and they were only halfway to Oregon Territory.

"Gee up!" called the guide as he cracked his whip. Lizzie grinned. She loved the loud crack that started everything moving. Men shouted and 30 wagons began to roll. The creaking of the wagon, the clatter of pots and pans tied to the sides — it was the music of the wagon train. Lizzie glanced back at Mama and baby Jeremiah.

With a wink, Papa handed Lizzie the reins. "You can drive the team," he said.

Lizzie felt the smooth leather. She watched the horses take one even step after another.

Papa chuckled. "You're as good at driving the team as I am."

"I wish I could crack the whip like you." Lizzie had tried, but she couldn't make it crack like Papa.

"Is Lizzie driving the team again?" asked Mama. She shook her head. "You're going to grow up as wild as a coyote," she said to Lizzie. "Where's your sunbonnet?" She frowned and told Lizzie to get into the wagon.

Lizzie knew better than to argue with Mama. She handed the reins to her father and climbed into the back. Jeremiah greeted her with a slobbery kiss.

That afternoon, the wagons camped down in a hollow by a stream. Papa got his gun and walked up the hill.

"Can I go with you?" Lizzie called out.

Mama scolded. "You may not. Young ladies do not hunt for jackrabbits."

Lizzie sighed. Mama never let her do anything fun.

"You watch Jeremiah for Mama," Papa said. "I'll be back soon."

Lizzie and Jeremiah made mudpies while Mama cooked bean stew. When it was thick and steaming, Mama called them for supper. Other families were sitting down to eat.

"We can't eat without Papa!" Lizzie said. Papa was always back by suppertime.

Mama's face looked worried. "Eat your stew," she said. "Papa will be back soon."

Lizzie ate, but each bite felt like a bee buzzing in her stomach. Jeremiah smeared beans on his face, but Lizzie couldn't laugh. She was too afraid. The wagon train would leave in the morning. What had happened to Papa?

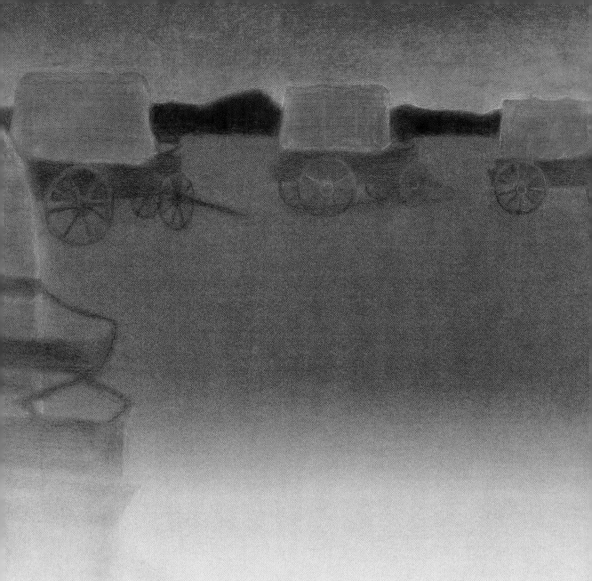

The stars were gleaming in the dark
sky when Mama helped Lizzie into her
nightgown. "Will Papa come?" she asked.

"Papa will never leave us," Mama said.
But her face was pale. Lizzie knew she was
scared, too.

Voices woke Lizzie in the night. "We

searched for a mile around the camp,"
Mr. Jenkins said. "But we couldn't find
him. We'll have to go tomorrow. We must
cross the mountains before the snow falls."

"I know," Mama said. Lizzie heard
footsteps walking away, and then soft crying.
Her heart beat extra fast. Mama never cried.

In the morning, Papa's bed was still empty. Mama's eyes were red from crying. Lizzie could not eat her oatmeal. Only Jeremiah smiled. He was too little to understand. All around were the sounds of people packing. Mama put everything into the wagon. Mr. Jenkins hitched up the horses.

The men talked and then Mr. Jenkins came to Mama. "We can't wait any longer," he said. "Come with us. It's dangerous to be alone on the prairie."

"We'll stay here," Mama said, her voice trembling.

Mr. Jenkins frowned. "We'll mark the trail," he said. He pointed to the mountains. "If he comes, you can follow our tracks."

Lizzie heard the whips crack. The wagons moved off and got smaller and smaller until all that was left was a dust cloud.

The crickets chirped in the long prairie grass. The birds swooped and called out. Lizzie sat with Jeremiah under a tree, blinking back tears. She felt like she had swallowed a stone. Where was Papa?

Suddenly she saw something crawling down the hill. Was it a wolf? "Mama!" she cried. Her legs were shaking. But Mama was already running toward it. It was Papa!

Lizzie took her father's hand. It was dry
and warm. His face was flushed.

"Rattlesnake bite," Mama said. "Look."
She pointed to Papa's torn pants.

Lizzie was so scared she could not say
a word.

They half-carried, half-dragged Papa to the wagon and got him into bed. "Get some cold water," Mama said. Lizzie filled the bucket at the stream. Mama soaked rags to wrap around Papa's swollen leg.

"Will Papa die?" Lizzie choked on the words.

Mama shook her head. "He's strong," she said. "But he'll be very sick. We can't follow the wagons now."

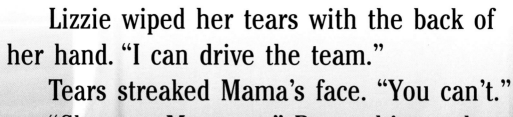

Lizzie wiped her tears with the back of her hand. "I can drive the team."

Tears streaked Mama's face. "You can't."

"She can, Margaret," Papa whispered. "Let her try. They're not too far ahead."

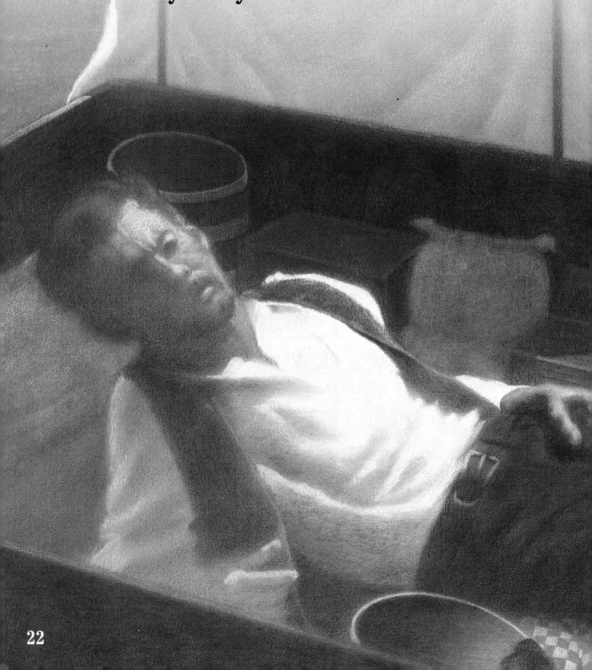

Lizzie's heart was pounding. Could she find the wagon train?

Mama looked at her. "Well Lizzie?"

Lizzie nodded. "I can do it."

Lizzie climbed into the seat and took the reins. She held the whip high in the air. She brought her arm back and then forward just like Papa.

"Crack!" went the whip.

"Gee-up!" shouted Lizzie. She steered the horses in the direction the train had taken. "We'll catch them," she said, "by tonight." When she looked back, Mama was smiling.